healthy cooking for your kids

healthy cooking for your kids

Sarah Banbery

This is a Parragon Book
First published in 2006

Parragon
Queen Street House
4 Queen Street
Bath BA1 1HE, UK

ISBN: 1-40545-019-3
Printed in China

Produced by the Bridgewater Book Company Ltd

Recipe photography: Clive Bozzard-Hill
Home economist: Sandra Baddeley
Illustrator: Anna Andrews

The Bridgewater Book Company would like to thank the following
for permission to reproduce copyright material: Jupiter Images
Corporation, front cover (bottom, second from left and second
from right) and pages 3, 5 (top), 6 (top left, middle left and
middle right), 8 (left and middle), 10 (bottom left, bottom middle
and bottom right), 12 (second from top, and bottom), 16 (top
left and bottom right), 17 and the front cover (second from left,
second from right); Image 100, page 9 (middle); and Laureen
March/Corbis, page 13.

Note
This book uses metric and imperial measurements. Follow the
same units of measurement throughout; do not mix metric and
imperial. All spoon measurements are level: teaspoons are assumed
to be 5 ml, and tablespoons are assumed to be 15 ml. Unless
otherwise stated, milk is assumed to be full fat, eggs and individual
vegetables such as potatoes are medium, and pepper is freshly
ground black pepper.

The times given for each recipe are an approximate guide only.
Preparation times differ according to the techniques used by
different people, and the cooking times may vary as a result of
the types of oven and other equipment used.

Whole nuts and seeds are not recommended for children under five
years of age. Nut butters and finely chopped or crushed nuts and
seeds are fine for babies of six months or older, unless there has
been a history of allergies to nuts or seeds within the family. If you
have any concerns, please discuss it with your health practitioner.

contents

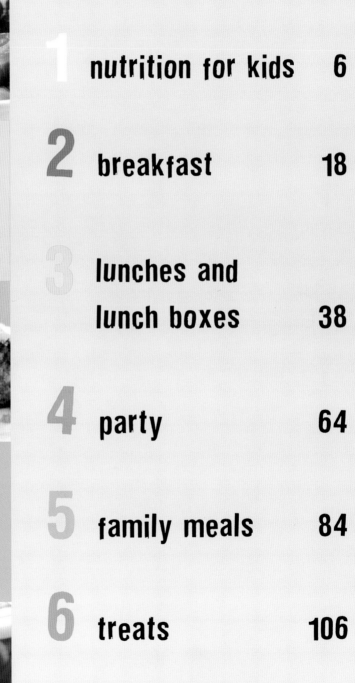

1

nutrition for kids

introduction

Healthy Cooking for Your Kids is designed to provide a range of delicious and easy recipes that will help you to give your child a balanced and nutritious diet. Good nutrition will not only benefit your child's health, but may also improve his or her behaviour and general well-being. Good – or bad – nutrition has an impact on the future health and development of your child and it is vital that healthy eating habits are established early, because they will then, most probably, last a lifetime.

What children eat directly affects their physical and mental development and is also crucial in fighting off illness. Ideally, children should have plenty of energy and a good capacity for mental concentration, as well as healthy teeth, skin and hair.

Children should be introduced to the widest variety of foods possible as soon as they begin eating solids in order to experience new flavours and textures and to develop an early interest in food. Regular meals and healthy snacks should provide a framework for a good diet with the right balance of nutrients and calorie content.

ESTABLISHING HEALTHY APPROACHES TO FOOD

Food can often become a battleground for parents and kids, so it is important to consider your own attitudes to food – your approach to food and eating, and that of the whole family, can affect the way your child views food. Try to avoid expressing a dislike for any particular food and make an effort to eat together as a family. Also avoid excluding any food from your child's diet, but keep certain foods such as processed foods to a minimum and when possible try to cook your child's food from scratch with fresh ingredients. Try not to use food as a bribe or a reward, but keep a balanced approach and avoid making certain foods more attractive by banning them. Once a food is banned, it inevitably becomes much more desirable. Try to include healthy 'treats' in your child's everyday diet to counteract the lure of unhealthy snack foods.

Presentation is often the key to interesting your child in new foods. For instance, boiled or steamed vegetables may be very healthy, but many children find them unappetizing, so think around the problem by 'hiding' vegetables in pasta sauces or on home-made pizzas. Taking kids along to farmers' markets or farm shops to see the range and variety of fruit and vegetables and where they come from may help interest your child in sampling them. Similarly, getting children involved in cooking is also a great way to encourage them to try new foods. The whole experience of planning, shopping, cooking and eating can be a fun way to help develop your child's palate, and will help to promote a healthy interest in food.

ACHIEVING A BALANCED DIET

A healthy diet is one that includes a rich diversity of foods, which will ensure that your child gets an adequate amount of all the major food groups. As a rough guide, your child should be having 2–4 portions (see page 15) of fruit, 3–5 portions of vegetables, 4–6 portions of grains/potatoes, 2–4 portions of calcium-rich foods, 2–4 portions of protein and 1–2 portions of healthy fats/oils each day. If this forms the basis for the way you feed your children, you will be providing them with the right balance of vitamins and minerals to keep them in good health.

Fruit and Vegetables

Include as many different kinds of fruit and vegetables as possible in your child's diet, because they are a rich source of energy, providing essential B vitamins, iron, minerals and fibre, as well as phytonutrients. Your child will get natural sugars from fresh and dried fruit, which should replace refined sugars in sweets, cakes and biscuits.

Grains and Potatoes

Try to include unrefined and wholegrain foods, and avoid 'white' or refined foods such as white bread and pasta. Granary and wholemeal bread and rolls, wholemeal flour, wholewheat pasta, porridge oats, potatoes, sweet potatoes and noodles are all good sources of iron, B vitamins and fibre, and will provide your child with energy.

Calcium-rich Foods

Growing children need calcium for strong bones and teeth and therefore require a range of calcium-rich foods in their diet, such as milk, soya milk, cheese, yogurt, tofu and canned oily fish such as sardines, as well as green leafy vegetables, nuts and seeds.

Protein

Protein is important for growth and development, and good sources include lean cuts of meat, chicken and turkey, fish, eggs, beans, lentils, nuts and seeds.

Fats/Oils

Avoid giving your child too many animal fats and concentrate on healthy oils that will provide omega-3 and omega-6 fats, which are important for brain development and good eyesight. Good sources are olive, rapeseed and sunflower oils, nut oils, nuts, seeds, oily fish such as mackerel and salmon, and avocados.

Salt and Sugar

It is important to monitor the amount of salt and sugar that your child is eating, because these can have adverse effects on your child's health. Salt contains sodium, and too much can lead to health problems such as raised blood pressure. Sugary foods contribute to tooth decay and have a high calorie content. Processed foods often have high levels of salt and sugar, so home-made food is the obvious way to control your child's intake of both.

Buy salt-reduced versions of foods such as tomato ketchup, soya sauce and stock, and replace crisps and salted nuts with dried fruit and raw nuts. Make your own pasta sauces and soups so that you can regulate the salt content.

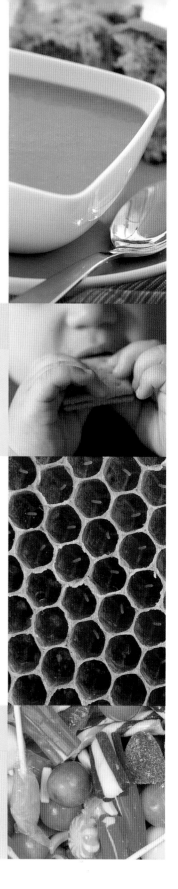

Recommended Levels of Salt

Under 7 years	no more than 3 g per day
7–10 years	no more than 5 g per day
11 years and older	no more than 6 g per day

Fizzy drinks, biscuits, cakes, sweets, chocolate and desserts are the obvious sources of sugar, but there may be high levels of sugar in processed foods such as ready-made pizzas, ready meals, cereals, canned foods, chicken nuggets and bottled sauces. Always check labels for sugar content and try to accustom your child to the natural sugar in fresh and dried fruit, honey and maple syrup.

Recommended Levels of Sugar

4–6 years	40 g per day
7–10 years	46 g per day
11–14 years	50 g per day

DEALING WITH INTOLERANCES AND ALLERGIES

Research into the increased incidence of food-related intolerance and allergies in children suggests that many may be controlled or eliminated by the right diet or simply restricting certain foods. Additives in food have been shown to provoke allergic reactions in some children and certain food colours and preservatives cause hyperactivity in others. If you suspect that your child may have a serious allergy, speak to your doctor. If there is a history of allergies in your family, avoid giving any nuts or nut products to children under the age of three and, in any case, whole nuts should not be given to the under-fives. Speak to your doctor about any concerns regarding allergies or intolerance symptoms, and take expert advice on compiling a diet that may restrict certain foods as necessary.

PRACTICAL STRATEGIES FOR HEALTHY EATING

Evidence suggests that a diet reliant on processed foods and with little fruit or vegetables can seriously affect a child's physical development as well as behaviour and concentration levels. While it may sometimes seem an effort to provide fresh, wholesome food, it really does make a difference to your child's health now and in the future. So having established that fresh food is best, how can you make sure that your child eats the foods that you choose? It is invaluable to have some strategies on hand for coping with problems associated with feeding your child the balanced diet he or she needs.

While the focus of this book is on healthy eating, it is important not to become obsessive and stressed over what your child is eating – you can't expect your child to like all foods, and as long as he or she is willing to try everything and then perhaps rejects the odd food, that should encourage a relaxed attitude to eating. As soon as your child reaches the age of one year, your goal should be to increase the variety of foods offered. For young children, bear in mind that the choice to eat or not may well just be a way of asserting their budding independence and becomes one of the few things in their lives over which they have any control.

Don't overload their plates – it is very off-putting for children to be presented with huge piles of food with you expecting them to eat it all. Instead, take a little time to present their food well and give them manageable portions – better that they ask for a little more than reject the whole plate. Don't press children to eat what they obviously dislike, but also don't give in to pressure to give them just what they want. Try not to make too much of an issue about it – if they refuse to eat what they are offered, simply remove it without a fuss and don't offer a replacement. However, continue to encourage them to try new flavours. Avoid commenting on what your children eat or discussing weight or calories in front of them. And do persevere – sometimes it may take three or four attempts before a child will develop a taste for a certain food and it can be the seemingly unlikely foods, such as olives, that become favourites. Try to avoid classifying foods as children's foods, since this excludes certain foods – 'adult' foods may appeal to many children, because they often like strong flavours.

Reaching the Five-a-day Target

Getting your child to eat the required five portions of fruit and vegetables a day may seem like a challenge, but once you realize that a portion is not too big, it will seem less daunting. A child's portion of fruit or vegetables is roughly the amount the child can hold in one hand – just increase the amount as the child grows. Then if you consider that you can actually often incorporate a significant amount of fruit or vegetables in one recipe, the five-a-day goal becomes far more realistic. For instance, the Creamy Tomato Soup on page 40 contains five different fresh vegetables, but since it is creamy and smooth, even the most veg-phobic child would struggle to identify them. Recipes like this, which incorporate vegetables rather than serving them as a side dish, tend to be more acceptable to children generally. So, if your child starts the day with a glass of fresh fruit juice, has chopped fruit for two snacks, and two or three more portions included in his or her meals, you're reached the target!

Be creative and add vegetables to kids' favourites such as mashed potatoes – you can easily add other root vegetables or puréed greens without much extra effort. You can also incorporate plenty of vegetables in Roast Vegetable Lasagne (see page 94), Burritos (see

page 88), Shepherd's Pie (see page 93) and all manner of other pies, as well as sandwich fillers, toppings and sauces. Children often prefer their vegetables raw, so colourful strips of raw vegetables are idea for lunch boxes, and fun 'Party Straws' of vegetables and fruit go down well (see page 83). Include fruit in as many desserts as possible – if your child loves ice cream, offer a small portion of organic ice cream with a home-made fruit purée, or make colourful and delicious Tropical Fruit Tarts or Mini Fruit Trifles (see pages 127 and 119). You can also make very healthy, pure fruit lollies by freezing fresh puréed fruit such as mango, strawberry and raspberry (see Yogurt Lollies on page 114).

Make sure you vary the fruit and vegetables, mixing up the colours. In fact, get your children to choose which fruit and vegetables they will have when shopping, but don't worry if they refuse some items, as long as they have a good mix. Letting your children help you choose what to buy and also helping themselves at the table makes them feel that they have some control.

HEALTHY EATING FOR LIFE

It is virtually impossible to regulate everything that your children eat, especially as they get older, but by encouraging good habits early on, you stand a much better chance of your children carrying them through to adulthood. By making even small changes to your children's diets, you can make a big difference, and putting in the effort at this early stage really does have its rewards and can influence the quality of your children's whole lives.

We all know that breakfast is an important meal, but it is doubly so for children. Breakfast is a vital meal for good nutrition and sets your child up for the day ahead. It should ideally include both complex carbohydrates and protein, and should really kick-start your child's metabolism.

2 breakfast

Many commercially produced breakfast cereals tend to have high levels of sugar and salt. If you do choose bought cereal, try to make sure that it has whole grains and no added sugar or salt, and add some chopped fresh or dried fruit. A home-made breakfast can be better for your child and doesn't have to be time consuming to prepare when you have a busy morning. Many of the recipes in this chapter can be put together quickly or made ahead, and will provide your child with a healthy, balanced start to the day.

Complex carbohydrates that release sugars into the bloodstream slowly will keep your child going throughout the morning and oats are a great source. They are featured here in home-made muesli, granola and porridge, which are easy to make and offer the opportunity to incorporate fruit and nuts to provide a good balance of nutrients for your child. A fruit muffin with added bran and a fruit smoothie also makes a great start to the day and your child can easily get involved in making these.

If your child asks for toast, Granary and wholemeal bread are the healthy options. Try out a variety of nut butters, which are available from health-food stores and some supermarkets – cashew nut or almond make good alternatives to peanut and work well with banana, or chopped apple or apricot. Choose fruit compotes with natural sugars – to make your own compote, just add a little honey or maple syrup to stewed fresh fruit such as apple and pear, or dark berries and strawberries.

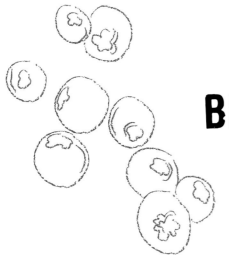

Blueberry Bran Muffins

Preheat the oven to 180°C/350°F/Gas Mark 4. Line 10 holes of a muffin tin with muffin paper cases.

Mix the flours, bran, baking powder, bicarbonate of soda and salt together in a bowl and stir in the sugar. Whisk the honey, egg and buttermilk together in a jug.

Pour the wet ingredients into the dry and stir briefly to combine. Don't overmix – the mixture should still be a little lumpy. Fold in the blueberries.

Spoon the mixture into the paper cases and bake in the preheated oven for 20 minutes until risen and lightly browned.

Remove the muffins from the oven and leave to cool in the tin. Serve warm or cold.

150 g/5½ oz white plain flour
100 g/3½ oz light brown
    self-raising flour
1 tbsp oat bran
2 tsp baking powder
½ tsp bicarbonate of soda
pinch of salt
50 g/1¾ oz demerara sugar
1 tbsp clear honey
1 large egg
200 ml/7 fl oz buttermilk
150 g/5½ oz fresh blueberries

Almond and Sultana Pancakes with Raspberries

Melt the butter in a small saucepan over a low heat.

Whisk the egg, buttermilk and vanilla extract together in a bowl, add the melted butter and stir to combine.

In a separate bowl, mix the flours, bicarbonate of soda and ground almonds together and then stir in the egg mixture and sultanas.

Heat half the oil in a large, non-stick frying pan and drop in 3–4 separate tablespoons of the batter – each will make a 10-cm/4-inch pancake, so don't overcrowd the pan. Cook for 2 minutes on each side, then remove from the pan and keep warm in a low oven while you cook the remaining pancakes. Use the remaining oil to do this.

Serve warm with the raspberries, scattered with the toasted almonds.

25 g/1 oz unsalted butter
1 large egg
300 ml/10 fl oz buttermilk
½ tsp vanilla extract
75 g/2¾ oz white plain flour
50 g/1¾ oz wholemeal plain flour
1 tsp bicarbonate of soda
25 g/1 oz ground almonds
75 g/2¾ oz sultanas
2 tsp vegetable oil
150 g/5½ oz fresh raspberries
50 g/1¾ oz toasted flaked almonds

Serves 1

Sunshine Toast

Using a biscuit cutter, cut a hole in the centre of the slice of bread, large enough to hold the egg.

Heat the oil in a non-stick frying pan and cook the mushrooms and tomato, cut-sides down, for 3–4 minutes until the mushrooms are beginning to brown. Turn the tomato over.

Make a space in the middle of the pan and add the bread. Crack the egg open and carefully pour it into the hole in the bread. Reduce the heat and cook slowly until cooked through.

Season everything to taste with pepper and serve the sunshine toast with the mushrooms and tomato alongside.

1 slice Granary or wholemeal bread
1 tbsp olive oil
2–3 mushrooms, sliced
1 tomato, halved
1 small egg
pepper

Serves 1

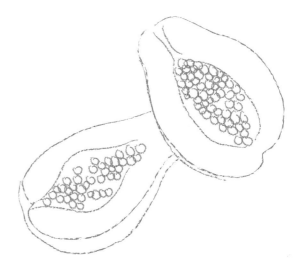

Fruit Smoothies

Place all the ingredients in a blender or food processor and process until combined and frothy. Pour into a tall glass and serve immediately.

Mango and Pawpaw
As for Berry, but substitute ½ stoned, peeled and chopped mango and ½ deseeded, peeled and chopped pawpaw for the berries and blackcurrants.

Banana, Peach and Strawberry
As for Berry, but substitute ½ peeled and sliced banana, ½ stoned, peeled and chopped peach, and 3 hulled strawberries for the berries and blackcurrants.

Berry
300 ml/10 fl oz full-fat milk
   or soya milk
2 tbsp natural yogurt
1 tbsp maple syrup
3 blackberries
50 g/1¾ oz blueberries
25 g/1 oz blackcurrants

Cereal Fruit Cupcakes

100 g/3½ oz unsalted butter

125 g/4½ oz clear honey

150 g/5½ oz porridge oats

50 g/1¾ oz unsweetened
   crispy rice

1 tbsp sesame seeds

100 g/3½ oz mixed dried fruit,
   such as pears, mangos, apples
   and cranberries, chopped

50 g/1¾ oz shelled pecan nuts,
   chopped

Melt the butter and honey in a small saucepan over a
low heat.

Mix the oats, crispy rice, sesame seeds, dried fruit and
chopped nuts together in a bowl, add the melted butter
and honey and stir to combine.

Spoon into 12 cake paper cases and press down well.
Chill for 6 hours before serving.

Crunchy Yogurt

This recipe will make more granola than you need. Make the granola in advance and keep it in an airtight container.

Preheat the oven to 180°C/350°F/Gas Mark 4.

Mix the oats and honey together in a bowl and spread out on a baking sheet. Bake in the preheated oven for 10–15 minutes, stirring a couple of times, until the oats are lightly browned, then remove from the oven and leave to cool.

Place the seeds in a mortar and briefly grind with a pestle to break them into smaller pieces. Mix with the cooled oats and the walnuts.

To assemble, put half the pear and mango in a glass and top with half the yogurt and a spoonful of granola. Repeat with the remaining fruit and yogurt and top with more granola.

200 g/7 oz rolled oats

2 tbsp clear honey

2 tbsp pumpkin seeds

2 tbsp sunflower seeds

2 tbsp chopped walnuts

1 small ripe pear, peeled, cored and chopped

½ ripe mango, stoned, peeled and chopped

125 g/4½ oz natural yogurt

Serves 4

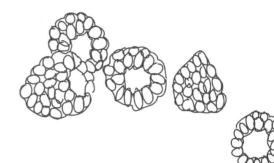

Bircher Muesli

The night before serving, mix the oats, wheatgerm and milk together in a bowl, cover with clingfilm and chill overnight.

To serve, stir the oat mixture, add the honey, yogurt and apple, and mix well.

Spoon into serving bowls, top with the nuts and berries and drizzle over a little more honey, or fruit purée, if using.

250 g/9 oz rolled oats

1 tbsp wheatgerm

200 ml/7 fl oz full-fat milk or soya milk

2 tbsp clear honey, plus extra for serving (optional)

2 tbsp natural yogurt

1 apple, peeled, cored and grated

150 g/5½ oz chopped nuts, such as macadamia nuts, cashew nuts or hazelnuts

mixed berries, such as blueberries, raspberries and strawberries

fruit purée, to serve (optional)

Apple and Hazelnut Bread

Grease and line a 450-g/1-lb loaf tin. Put 100 ml/3½ fl oz of the warm water in a jug, stir in the sugar and yeast and leave for 15 minutes.

Mix the flours, salt, nuts and dried and fresh apple together in a large bowl. Make a well in the centre, pour in the yeast mixture and gradually work into the flour mixture. Mix in the remaining warm water and bring together to form a soft dough.

Turn out onto a floured work surface and knead briefly. Shape the dough into a rectangle and place in the prepared tin. Cover with a warm, damp cloth and set aside in a warm place for 40 minutes until the dough has risen.

Meanwhile, preheat the oven to 200°C/400°F/ Gas Mark 6. Remove the cloth and bake the loaf in the preheated oven for 40 minutes. Carefully lift out of the tin and return the loaf to the oven, upside down, for 10–15 minutes – the loaf should sound hollow when tapped on the bottom.

Remove from the oven and leave to cool on a wire rack. Slice and serve spread with honey, and sliced banana or nut butter. Store wrapped in foil for up to three days, or freeze for up to a month.

butter, for greasing

350 ml/12 fl oz warm water

1 tsp golden caster sugar

1 x 7-g/⅛-oz sachet easy-blend
    dried yeast

400 g/14 oz white plain flour,
    plus extra for dusting

400 g/14 oz light brown self-raising
    flour

½ tsp sea salt

125 g/4½ oz toasted hazelnuts,
    chopped

50 g/1¾ oz dried apple, chopped

1 eating apple, grated

To serve
honey
sliced banana or nut butter

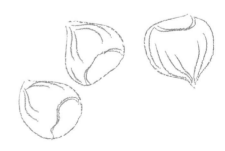

Mini Cheese and Herb Muffins

100 g/3½ oz baby spinach leaves

75 g/2¾ oz butter

35 g/1¼ oz Parmesan cheese, finely grated

1 tbsp chopped fresh herbs, such as chives, parsley or tarragon

100 g/3½ oz white plain flour

100 g/3½ oz light brown self-raising flour

½ tsp bicarbonate of soda

pinch of salt

2 tsp baking powder

1 large egg

200 ml/7 fl oz buttermilk

Preheat the oven to 200°C/400°F/Gas Mark 6. Line two 12-hole mini muffin tins with mini muffin paper cases.

Put the spinach in a colander and pour boiling water from a kettle over the leaves to wilt them. Leave to cool, then squeeze all the liquid out until the spinach is very dry. Chop finely.

Melt the butter in a small saucepan over a low heat, then leave to cool. Mix the cheese, herbs, flours, bicarbonate of soda, salt and baking powder together in a bowl, then stir in the spinach.

Whisk the melted butter with the egg and buttermilk in a jug, pour into the dry ingredients and stir briefly to combine. Don't overmix – the mixture should still be a little lumpy.

Spoon a teaspoon of the mixture into each of the paper cases and bake in the preheated oven for 12 minutes.

Remove from the oven and leave to cool in the tin. Serve warm or cold.

Buttered Cinnamon Apples on Fruit Toast

1 tbsp unsalted butter

½ tsp ground cinnamon

1 apple, cored and sliced

1 slice fruit bread

maple syrup, to serve

Melt the butter in a saucepan over a low heat and stir in the cinnamon. Add the apple and stir well to coat.

Preheat the grill and line the grill pan with foil. Spread the buttered apple over the grill pan. Cook under the grill until the apple is just beginning to brown. Toast the fruit bread and serve with the apple piled on top, drizzled with a little maple syrup.

Serves 1

Baked Eggs with Ham and Tomato

Preheat the oven to 180°C/350°F/Gas Mark 4. Heat the oil in a saucepan and cook the leek for 5–6 minutes until soft.

Place the leek in the bottom of a ramekin and top with the ham. Crack and pour in the egg, then top with the cheese and tomato.

Bake in the preheated oven for 10 minutes until the egg is set. Remove the ramekin from the oven, leave to cool a little, wrap in a cloth and serve.

1 tsp olive oil

½ small leek, chopped

2 slices wafer-thin ham, chopped

1 egg

25 g/1 oz Cheddar cheese, grated

2 slices tomato

Serves 1

Fruity Maple Porridge

Mix the milk and oats together in a saucepan and cook over a medium heat, stirring, for 8–10 minutes.

Serve drizzled with the maple syrup and topped with the fresh fruit, with a little more milk if needed.

To make a breakfast brûlée, preheat the grill and put the chopped fruit in the bottom of a ramekin. Top with the cooked porridge and a spoonful of brown sugar and place under the grill until the sugar has melted and caramelized. Chill before serving.

175 ml/6 fl oz full-fat milk or
     soya milk, plus extra for serving
     (optional)
50 g/1¾ oz porridge oats
1 tbsp maple syrup or clear honey
mixed fresh fruit, such as apples,
     pears, bananas, peaches,
     mangoes, strawberries and
     raspberries, prepared and
     chopped

Coming up with a varied, interesting and tempting lunch or lunch box for your child is a daily challenge. A healthy and delicious lunch box that is filling, nutritious yet also enjoyable is important, because it should provide your child with the energy to sustain him or her right through the afternoon.

3 lunches and lunch boxes

Kids' lunch boxes should contain healthy foods that will nourish them and keep them energized. Lunch should provide a third of your child's daily intake of protein, carbohydrate, fibre, vitamins and minerals, so it needs to be really appetizing and variety is the watchword. A healthy lunch box should include a portion of fresh fruit and vegetables, plus one portion each of protein, carbohydrate and a calcium-rich food such as cheese, yogurt or milk. If you pack some fruit, and a no-added-sugar fruit drink or water, plus a healthy sandwich or salad, your child will have a tasty, balanced meal. Home-made noodle, pasta and couscous salads in pots are great served cold in a lunch box with plenty of added vegetables, and home-made scones and cookies are a sweet treat. However, as this chapter shows, all sorts of other foods work well in lunch boxes. There are also many good foods pre-packaged to fit into lunch boxes, such as mini tubs of fresh and dried fruit, mini cheese portions and small pots of yogurt or fromage frais. Nuts and vegetable crisps make healthy substitutes for potato crisps. Besides fruit juice or water to drink, a fruit smoothie or a milkshake is a good option – avoid fizzy canned drinks or fruit squashes with sugar.

Getting children involved in planning and preparing lunch can make a difference to the way they feel about eating it. Baking biscuits or tartlets at the weekend or planning the toppings for home-made muffin pizzas can be fun and gets children involved in thinking about food and cooking.

Creamy Tomato Soup

15 g/½ oz butter

½ red onion, finely chopped

1 leek, chopped

1 garlic clove, crushed

1 carrot, peeled and grated

1 potato, peeled and grated

300 ml/10 fl oz low-salt
    vegetable stock

500 g/1 lb 2 oz ripe tomatoes,
    peeled, deseeded and chopped

1 tbsp tomato purée

150 ml/5 fl oz full-fat milk

sea salt and pepper

snipped chives, to garnish
    (optional)

Granary rolls, to serve

Melt the butter in a large saucepan over a low heat and cook the onion, leek and garlic for 10 minutes, or until very soft but not browned.

Add the carrot and potato and cook for 5 minutes. Add the stock and bring up to simmering point.

Add the tomatoes and tomato purée and season to taste with salt and pepper. Simmer for 15 minutes until the vegetables are very soft. Add the milk and warm through, then transfer the soup to a blender or food processor and process until very smooth. You can pass the soup through a sieve at this stage, if you like.

Return the soup to the rinsed-out saucepan and reheat gently. Garnish the soup with snipped chives, if desired, and serve with Granary rolls.

Serves 2

Sesame Noodle Stir-fry

Mix the vinegar, soy sauce, tomato ketchup, orange juice and honey together in a jug, add the cornflour and stir until well combined.

Heat the oil in a non-stick frying pan and stir-fry the chicken strips for 3–4 minutes. Add the vegetables and stir-fry for 4–5 minutes.

Add the cornflour mixture and bring to the boil, stirring constantly, then reduce the heat and simmer for 1 minute until thickened.

Meanwhile, prepare the noodles according to the packet instructions, drain and add to the pan along with the sesame seeds. Mix well. Serve hot or cold.

1 tsp red wine vinegar

1 tbsp low-salt soy sauce

1 tbsp low-sugar and -salt tomato ketchup

2 tbsp orange juice

1 tsp clear honey

1 tsp cornflour

1 tbsp vegetable oil

100 g/3½ oz skinless, boneless chicken breast, cut into strips

2 spring onions, finely sliced

55 g/2 oz baby sweetcorn, halved lengthways

1 carrot, cut into thin batons

½ red pepper, deseeded and chopped

½ courgette, chopped

50 g/1¾ oz bean thread noodles

2 tsp sesame seeds

Pitta Pockets with Hummus and Salad

400 g/14 oz canned chickpeas,
   drained and liquid reserved

1 garlic clove, chopped

3 tbsp olive oil

2 tbsp tahini

juice of ½ lemon

pinch of paprika

2–4 pitta breads

1 tsp vinegar

½ tsp Dijon mustard

¼ iceberg lettuce, finely shredded

1 spring onion, chopped

½ yellow pepper, deseeded
   and chopped

1 large tomato, deseeded
   and chopped

5-cm/2-inch piece cucumber,
   chopped

1 carrot, peeled and grated

pepper

To make the hummus, put the chickpeas, garlic, 2 tablespoons of the oil, the tahini, lemon juice and a little of the chickpea liquid in a blender or food processor and blend until smooth and creamy. Season to taste with pepper and the paprika.

If serving at home, heat the pitta breads according to the packet instructions and split each one to create a pocket.

To make the dressing, whisk the remaining oil with the vinegar and mustard, and pepper to taste, in a jug.

Mix all the salad ingredients together in a bowl, add the dressing and toss well to coat. Smear the inside of the pitta pockets with the hummus, fill with the salad and serve. For a lunch box, smear the inside of the unheated pitta pockets with hummus, fill with the undressed salad and wrap well in foil.

Serves 4

Souffléd Baked Potatoes

Preheat the oven to 200°C/400°F/Gas Mark 6. Rub the oil all over the potatoes, place on a baking sheet and bake in the preheated oven for 1 hour, or until the flesh is soft.

Remove the potatoes from the oven, cut in half lengthways and carefully scoop out the flesh into a bowl, keeping the skins intact. Set the skins aside.

Add the milk, butter, Cheddar cheese and egg yolk to the potato and mash well. Season to taste with salt and pepper. Mix in the ham.

In a separate, grease-free bowl, whisk the egg white until stiff, then fold into the potato mixture.

Pile the potato mixture back into the skins and sprinkle over the Parmesan cheese. Return to the oven and bake for 20 minutes. Serve with salad.

1 tbsp olive oil

2 baking potatoes, scrubbed

2 tbsp full-fat milk

25 g/1 oz butter

25 g/1 oz Cheddar or Gruyère
cheese, grated

1 large egg, separated

2 slices ham, cooked turkey
or unsmoked bacon, chopped

2 tbsp finely grated Parmesan
cheese

sea salt and pepper

salad, to serve

Tortillas with Tuna, Egg and Sweetcorn

1 tbsp natural yogurt

1 tsp olive oil

½ tsp white wine vinegar

½ tsp Dijon mustard

1 large egg, hard-boiled
   and cooled

200 g/7 oz canned tuna in spring
   water, drained

200 g/7 oz canned no-added-sugar
   sweetcorn kernels, drained

2 wholemeal flour tortillas

1 punnet mustard cress

pepper

To make the dressing, whisk the yogurt, oil, vinegar and mustard, and pepper to taste, in a jug until emulsified and smooth.

Shell the egg, separate the yolk and the white, then mash the yolk and chop the white finely. Mash the tuna with the egg and dressing, then mix in the sweetcorn.

Spread the filling equally over the 2 tortillas and sprinkle over the mustard and cress. Fold in one end and roll up. Wrap in foil for a packed lunch.

Chicken and Apple Bites

1 apple, peeled, cored and
  grated
2 skinless, boneless chicken
  breasts, cut into chunks
½ red onion, finely chopped
1 tbsp finely chopped fresh
  parsley
50 g/1¾ oz fresh wholemeal
  breadcrumbs
1 tbsp concentrated chicken
  stock
wholemeal flour, for coating
groundnut oil, for
  shallow-frying

Spread the apple out on a clean tea towel and press out all the excess moisture.

Put the chicken, apple, onion, parsley, breadcrumbs and stock in a food processor and pulse briefly until well combined.

Spread the flour out on a plate. Divide the mixture into 20 mini portions, shape each portion into a ball and roll in the flour.

Heat a little oil in a non-stick frying pan over a medium heat and cook the balls for 5–8 minutes, or until golden brown all over and cooked through. Remove and drain on kitchen paper. Serve hot, or cold for a lunch box.

Makes 6

Mini Muffin Pizzas

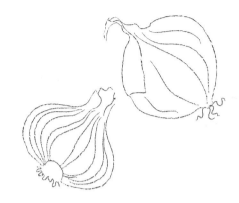

Toast the muffins until golden, then leave to cool.

Mix the tomato purée and pesto together in a small bowl and spread equally over the muffin halves.

Heat the oil in a non-stick frying pan and then cook the onion, mushrooms and courgette until soft and beginning to brown.

Preheat the grill to high. Divide the vegetables between the muffins and top with the ham and then the cheese.

Cook under the grill for 3–4 minutes until the cheese is melted and browned. Serve hot or cold.

3 wholemeal bread muffins, halved

2 tbsp tomato purée

2 tbsp pesto

1 tbsp olive oil

½ red onion, thinly sliced

3 mushrooms, sliced

½ courgette, thinly sliced

2–3 slices ham or 6 slices salami

100 g/3½ oz grated Cheddar cheese
   or 6 slices mozzarella cheese

Serves 6

Spanish Omelette

Cook the potatoes in a saucepan of boiling water for 8–12 minutes until tender. Drain and leave to cool, then slice.

Heat the oil in an 18–20-cm/7–8-inch frying pan with a heatproof handle and cook the sliced onion and red pepper until soft. Add the tomatoes and cook for a further minute.

Add the potatoes to the pan and spread out evenly. Beat the eggs, milk and cheese, and salt and pepper to taste, in a bowl and pour over the potato mixture. Cook for 4–5 minutes until the eggs are set underneath.

Meanwhile, preheat the grill to high. Place the frying pan under the grill and cook the omelette for a further 3–4 minutes until the eggs are set.

Leave to cool, then cut into wedges and wrap in foil for a lunch box.

200 g/7 oz new potatoes

1 tbsp olive oil

1 onion, thinly sliced

1 red pepper, deseeded and thinly sliced

2 tomatoes, peeled, deseeded and chopped

6 large eggs

1 tbsp milk

2 tbsp finely grated Parmesan cheese

sea salt and pepper

Makes 12

Apple and Carrot Muffins

Preheat the oven to 180°C/350°F/Gas Mark 4. Line 12 holes of a muffin tin with muffin paper cases.

150 g/5½ oz white plain flour

100 g/3½ oz light brown self-
raising flour

2 tsp baking powder

½ tsp bicarbonate of soda

pinch of sea salt

½ tsp ground nutmeg

1 apple, peeled, cored and grated

½ carrot, peeled and grated

4 tbsp clear honey

1 large egg, beaten

200 ml/7 fl oz buttermilk

4 tbsp demerara sugar

Mix the flours, baking powder, bicarbonate of soda, salt and nutmeg together in a bowl.

In a separate bowl, mix the apple and carrot together. Stir in the honey and egg, then the buttermilk and sugar. Pour this mixture into the dry ingredients and stir briefly to combine. Don't overmix – the mixture should still be a little lumpy.

Spoon the mixture into the paper cases and bake in the preheated oven for 20 minutes.

Remove from the oven and leave to cool in the tin. Serve warm or cold.

Sandwiches and Wraps

Use as many varieties of breads as possible to add interest. Choose Granary or wholemeal bread or rolls, wholemeal pitta breads, tortillas, rye bread, fruit or nut breads and wholegrain bagels and crispbreads, but do not use white processed bread. Some younger children like sandwiches cut into novelty shapes, but you can also make double-decker sandwiches with three different types of wholegrain breads, or use mini pitta breads, breadsticks or tortilla wraps. At home, use Little Gem lettuce boats to hold the fillings and add as much chopped salad as possible. Also include tubs of cherry tomatoes, batons of celery, peppers or carrot, or use straws to make mini vegetable or fruit kebabs. Above all, keep it varied, interesting and easy to pack and eat.

Try some of the following fillings for sandwiches, mixing and matching to add variety.

cream cheese or goat's cheese with snipped chives or chopped spring onion

mashed canned salmon, tuna, sardines or crab with or without mayonnaise

mashed banana

dried fruit, such as apricot, mango or pear, chopped

canned no-added-sugar sweetcorn kernels

chopped hard-boiled egg

avocado

nut butters

honey

hummus

shredded cooked chicken or turkey

lean ham

cooked prawns

grated carrot and cheese

vegetable pâté

bean pâté

cottage cheese

ricotta cheese

guacamole

Pasta Salad

100 g/3½ oz small wholewheat
  pasta

2 tbsp olive oil, plus extra if
  needed

1 tbsp mayonnaise

1 tbsp natural yogurt

2 tbsp pesto

200 g/7 oz canned tuna in spring
  water, drained and flaked

200 g/7 oz canned no-added-sugar
  sweetcorn kernels, drained

2 tomatoes, peeled, deseeded
  and chopped

½ green pepper, deseeded
  and chopped

½ avocado, stoned, peeled
  and chopped

sea salt and pepper

Cook the pasta in a large saucepan of boiling water for
8–10 minutes until only just tender. Drain, return to the
saucepan and add half the oil. Toss well to coat, then
cover and leave to cool.

Whisk the mayonnaise, yogurt and pesto together in a
jug, adding a little oil if needed to achieve the desired
consistency. Add a pinch of salt and season to taste
with pepper.

Mix the cooled pasta with the tuna, sweetcorn, tomatoes,
green pepper and avocado, add the dressing and toss
well to coat.

Makes 12

125 g/4½ oz butter, diced and
    chilled, plus extra for greasing
150 g/5½ oz white plain flour, plus
    extra for dusting
100 g/3½ oz wholemeal plain flour
1 tbsp finely grated Parmesan
    cheese
about 1 tbsp cold water
24 cherry tomatoes
1 tbsp olive oil
200 ml/7 fl oz full-fat milk
50 g/1¾ oz Cheddar cheese, grated
100 g/3½ oz ricotta cheese
sea salt and pepper

Cherry Tomato and Cheese Tartlets

Lightly grease a 12-hole muffin tin with butter. Put 125 g/4½ oz of the white flour in a food processor with all the wholemeal flour, a pinch of salt and 100 g/3½ oz of the butter, and pulse until the mixture resembles breadcrumbs. Tip into a large bowl and stir in the Parmesan cheese. Alternatively, mix the flours with the salt in a large bowl, add the butter and rub in with your fingertips until the mixture resembles breadcrumbs. Then stir in the Parmesan cheese. Add 1 tablespoon cold water, stir and bring the mixture together to form a dough, adding a little more cold water if needed. Turn out onto a floured work surface and knead briefly.

Divide the dough into 12 pieces, roll out each piece into a 12-cm/4½-inch round and use to line the muffin holes. Chill for 30 minutes. Meanwhile, preheat the oven to 200°C/400°F/ Gas Mark 6. Remove the muffin tin from the refrigerator and line each pastry case with baking paper and baking beans. Bake blind in the preheated oven for 10 minutes, then remove from the oven. Lift out the paper and beans and set the pastry cases aside.

Put the tomatoes in a roasting tin and drizzle over the oil. Roast in the oven for 5 minutes. Meanwhile, melt the remaining 25 g/1 oz butter in a saucepan over a low heat. Stir in the remaining white flour and cook, stirring constantly, for 2–3 minutes. Gradually stir in the milk and cook, stirring constantly, until the sauce is thick and smooth. Season to taste with salt and pepper and stir in the Cheddar and ricotta cheeses.

Put 2 tomatoes in each pastry case and then divide the cheese sauce between the tartlets. Bake in the oven for 15 minutes until golden.

Apricot and Sunflower Seed Cookies

100 g/3½ oz unsalted butter, softened

50 g/1¾ oz demerara sugar

1 tbsp maple syrup

1 tbsp honey, plus extra for brushing

1 large egg, beaten

100 g/3½ oz white plain flour, plus extra for dusting

150 g/5½ oz wholemeal plain flour

1 tbsp oat bran

50 g/1¾ oz ground almonds

1 tsp ground cinnamon

75 g/2¾ oz ready-to-eat dried apricots, chopped

25 g/1 oz sunflower seeds

Beat the softened butter with the sugar in a large bowl until light and fluffy. Beat in the maple syrup and honey, then the egg.

Add the flours and oat bran, then the almonds and mix well. Add the cinnamon, apricots and seeds and, with floured hands, mix to a firm dough. Wrap in clingfilm and chill for 30 minutes.

Preheat the oven to 180°C/350°F/Gas Mark 4. Roll out the dough on a lightly floured work surface to 1 cm/½ inch thick. Using a 6-cm/2½-inch biscuit cutter, cut out 20 rounds, re-rolling the trimmings where possible, and place on a baking sheet. Brush with a little extra honey and bake in the preheated oven for 15 minutes until golden. Remove from the oven and leave to cool on a wire rack.

Makes 12

Orange and Banana Scones

Preheat the oven to 200°C/400°F/Gas Mark 6. Lightly oil a baking sheet.

Mix the flours, baking powder and cinnamon together in a large bowl, add the butter and rub in with your fingertips until the mixture resembles breadcrumbs. Stir in the sugar. Make a well in the middle and pour in the milk, add the banana and orange rind and mix to a soft dough. The dough will be quite wet.

Turn out the dough onto a lightly floured work surface and, adding a little more flour if needed, roll out to 2 cm/¾ inch thick. Using a 6-cm/2½-inch biscuit cutter, cut out 12 scones, re-rolling the trimmings where possible, and place them on the prepared baking sheet. Brush with milk and bake in the preheated oven for 10–12 minutes.

Remove from the oven and leave to cool slightly, then halve the scones and fill with the raspberries.

sunflower oil, for oiling
150 g/5½ oz white self-raising flour,
    plus extra for dusting, and
    rolling if needed
150 g/5½ oz light brown self-
    raising flour
1 tsp baking powder
½ tsp ground cinnamon
75 g/2¾ oz unsalted butter, diced
    and chilled
50 g/1¾ oz demerara sugar
150 ml/5 fl oz full-fat milk,
    plus extra for brushing
1 ripe banana, peeled and mashed
finely grated rind of 1 orange
150 g/5½ oz fresh raspberries,
    lightly mashed

Couscous Salad with Roasted Butternut Squash

2 tbsp honey

4 tbsp olive oil

1 butternut squash, peeled,
    deseeded and cut into
    2-cm/¾-inch chunks

250 g/9 oz couscous

400 ml/14 fl oz low-salt
    vegetable stock

½ cucumber, diced

1 courgette, diced

1 red pepper, deseeded and diced

juice of ½ lemon

2 tbsp chopped fresh parsley

sea salt and pepper

Preheat the oven to 190°C/375°F/Gas Mark 5. Mix half the honey with 1 tablespoon of the oil in a large bowl, add the squash and toss well to coat. Tip into a roasting tin and roast in the preheated oven for 30–40 minutes until soft and golden.

Meanwhile, put the couscous in a heatproof bowl. Heat the stock in a saucepan and pour over the couscous, cover and leave for 3 minutes. Add 1 tablespoon of the remaining oil and fork through, then stir in the diced cucumber, courgette and red pepper. Re-cover and keep warm.

Whisk the remaining honey and oil with the lemon juice in a jug and season to taste with salt and pepper. Stir the mixture through the couscous.

To serve, top the couscous with the roasted squash and sprinkle with the parsley.

Serves 4

Creamy Pasta Bake

Preheat the oven to 190°C/375°F/Gas Mark 5. Cook the wholewheat pasta in a large saucepan of boiling water for 10–12 minutes until just tender, then drain.

Meanwhile, heat the oil in a large frying pan and cook the mushrooms until beginning to brown. Boil or steam the broccoli until just cooked, then drain.

Add the chicken to the mushrooms and stir well. Blend the cornflour with a little milk in a jug, then gradually add the remaining milk, stirring constantly. Pour into the pan, add the crème fraîche and warm through, stirring.

Add the pasta and broccoli to the frying pan and season to taste with salt and pepper. Mix well, then transfer to a baking dish, top with the cheese and bake in the preheated oven for 15 minutes. Serve hot.

175 g/6 oz wholewheat pasta
    shells
1 tbsp olive oil
125 g/4½ oz button mushrooms,
    quartered
1 broccoli crown, broken into
    small florets
2 cooked skinless, boneless
    chicken breasts, shredded
1 tbsp cornflour
200 ml/7 fl oz milk
125 ml/4 fl oz half-fat crème
    fraîche
50 g/1¾ oz Cheddar cheese, grated
sea salt and pepper

Preparing healthy party food may be the biggest culinary challenge of all for parents. The combination of excitement, friends, gifts and sugar overload has led to many a party meltdown. Most traditional party foods are fairly unhealthy, and while you don't want to deprive your child of treats, there are fun ways to make healthy foods appealing for the partygoers.

4 party

This chapter offers a variety of appetizing and delicious foods that work well at parties and even includes a healthy birthday cake that is nevertheless attractive. Children tend to like finger food at parties and want a colourful and tempting choice of items, so offer a good range of bite-sized morsels, and the right balance of savoury and sweet foods. Offer only the savoury options at first and bring out the sweet ones after the kids have eaten at least some of the savoury. Try starting the party off by giving each child an individual party box, labelled with his or her name, which contains a selection of finger foods, such as a cocktail sausage, chicken drumstick, mini quiche, a couple of pinwheel sandwiches and a savoury straw. Kids can have these before sitting down at the table for the sweet treats. Fruit cocktails or smoothies decorated with umbrellas and fresh fruit are entertaining and a healthy party substitute for fizzy drinks. If you offer sandwiches, make them fingers, pinwheels or in novelty shapes to encourage the kids to try them. Use as many healthy fillings as possible.

Presentation is important in tempting children to eat, so think carefully about this aspect of party food. Use colourful paper plates, napkins and tablecloths, and consider choosing an imaginative theme to bring all the elements together.

Honey Sesame Sausages

1 tbsp olive oil, plus extra
for oiling
2 tbsp clear honey
24 lean organic cocktail pork
sausages
2 tbsp sesame seeds

Preheat the oven to 190°C/375°F/Gas Mark 5. Brush a non-stick baking sheet with a little oil and place in the oven.

Whisk the honey and oil together in a large bowl, add the sausages and toss well to coat.

Spread the sesame seeds out on a large piece of greaseproof paper and roll each sausage in the seeds until well coated.

Remove the baking sheet from the oven and place the sausages on it. Bake the sausages in the preheated oven for 10 minutes. Turn the sausages over and bake for a further 10–15 minutes until well browned and sticky.

Serve warm or cold, either on sticks or in individual bowls.

Makes 12

Mini Crunchy Banana Sandwiches

Preheat the oven to 190°C/375°F/Gas Mark 5. Mix the butter and cinnamon together in a bowl until well combined. Spread sparingly on both sides of the bread.

Using novelty biscuit cutters, cut out fun shapes from the bread slices, such as stars, moons, and so on.

Place the shapes on a baking sheet and bake in the preheated oven for 8–10 minutes until golden. Remove from the oven and leave to cool.

Just before serving, mix the banana and chocolate together and use to sandwich the shapes together.

100 g/3½ oz unsalted butter,
    softened
1 teaspoon ground cinnamon
6 slices wholemeal bread
1 large, ripe banana, thinly sliced
25 g/1 oz plain chocolate
    (minimum 70% cocoa solids),
    shaved

Sticky Drumsticks with Cucumber Salad

6 organic chicken drumsticks

2 tbsp maple syrup

2 tbsp low-salt soy sauce

1 tsp sesame oil

½ cucumber, thinly sliced

2 spring onions, thinly sliced

sea salt

Preheat the oven to 190°C/375°F/Gas Mark 5. Trim the chicken drumsticks of any excess skin and pat dry with kitchen paper.

Mix the maple syrup, soy sauce and sesame oil in a large bowl. Add the chicken drumsticks and toss well to coat.

Place the chicken drumsticks on a non-stick baking sheet and roast in the preheated oven for 30–40 minutes, basting occasionally, until the chicken is tender, well browned and sticky, and the juices run clear when a skewer is inserted into the thickest part of the meat.

Meanwhile, put the cucumber in a colander and sprinkle with a little salt. Leave for 10 minutes until the juices have drained out. Pat dry with kitchen paper and mix with the spring onions.

Serve the chicken hot or cold with the cucumber salad.

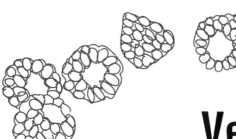

Very Berry Jelly

1 x 12-g/½-oz sachet of sugar-free
raspberry or strawberry jelly
200 ml/7 fl oz unsweetened
cranberry juice
500 g/1 lb 2 oz raspberries,
strawberries, redcurrants,
blueberries and blackberries

Make up the jelly according to the packet instructions, but use the cranberry juice to replace some of the water.

Place a mixture of berries in the bottom of individual serving glasses or plastic cups and pour over the jelly. Chill for 6 hours until firmly set.

Serve decorated with more berries.

To make a striped layer jelly, use 2 contrastingly coloured jellies. Put a quarter of the berries in a bowl or jelly mould and top with half of one jelly. Chill until just set, then add more berries and half of the contrasting jelly. Chill as before. Repeat twice more with the remaining jelly, alternating the colours. Chill until firmly set.

Serves 6–8

Avocado Dip with Spicy Potato Skins

Preheat the oven to 190°C/375°F/Gas Mark 5. Rub the potatoes with 1 tablespoon of the oil, place on a baking sheet and bake in the preheated oven for 1–1½ hours until the flesh is soft.

Remove the potatoes from the oven, cut in half lengthways and carefully scoop out the flesh into a bowl, but leave a generous 1 cm/½ inch of the potato on the skins. You can use the potato flesh to make mash.

Cut the skins into wedges. Put the remaining oil in a large bowl with the garlic, paprika and chilli flakes and mix until well combined. Season sparingly with salt and pepper.

Toss the potato wedges in the spicy oil, spread out on the baking sheet and bake in the oven for 20 minutes until the skins are brown and crisp.

Meanwhile, to make the dip, in a separate bowl mash the avocado with the lemon juice, then mash in the cheese and potato flesh until well combined and smooth.

Serve the spicy skins warm, piled up, with little pots of the dip.

4 large baking potatoes, scrubbed

3 tbsp olive oil

1 garlic clove, crushed

¼ tsp paprika

½ tsp dried chilli flakes (optional)

2 ripe avocados, stoned and peeled

juice of ½ lemon

150 g/5½ oz soft goat's cheese

sea salt and pepper

Makes 12 slices

Party Carrot Cake

Preheat the oven to 180°C/350°F/Gas Mark 4. Grease and line a 20-cm/8-inch round cake tin.

Mix the flours, baking powder, salt and spices together in a large bowl and stir in the sugar and walnuts. Add the bananas and carrots and mix well.

In a separate bowl, mix the oil, eggs and vanilla extract together. Pour into the flour mixture and mix well to combine. Spoon the mixture into the prepared cake tin and level the surface.

Bake in the preheated oven for 1 hour, then test to see if it is cooked by inserting a skewer into the centre. If it comes out clean, the cake is done. If not, bake for a further 10 minutes and test again. Remove from the oven and leave to cool in the tin.

Turn the cake out onto a serving plate and spread with the cream cheese, if using. To make mini 'carrots' for decoration, cut each apricot in half horizontally and cut the snake into twelve 3-cm/1¼-inch lengths. Use 2 pieces of the snake to form the carrot 'stem' and roll an apricot half around it to form a mini carrot. Repeat until you have 6 'carrots'. Use to decorate the cake.

unsalted butter, for greasing

125 g/4½ oz light brown self-raising flour

100 g/3½ oz white self-raising flour

2 tsp baking powder

pinch of sea salt

1 tsp ground cinnamon

1 tsp ground nutmeg

125 g/4½ oz demerara sugar

50 g/1¾ oz shelled walnuts, chopped

2 ripe bananas, peeled and mashed

100 g/3½ oz carrots, peeled and finely grated

150 ml/5 fl oz light sunflower oil

2 eggs, beaten

1 tsp vanilla extract

cream cheese (optional)

3 ready-to-eat dried apricots

green confectionery snake

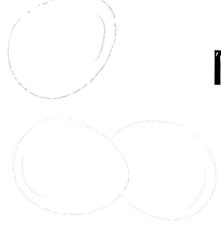

Mini Quiches

Preheat the oven to 200°C/400°F/Gas Mark 6. Lightly grease a 12-hole muffin tin with butter.

Put the flours, butter and a pinch of salt in a food processor and pulse until the mixture resembles breadcrumbs. Add the egg yolk and pulse again to form a dough, adding a little cold water if necessary. Alternatively, mix the flours and salt together in a large bowl, add the butter and rub in with your fingertips until the mixture resembles breadcrumbs. Mix in the egg yolk to form a dough, adding a little cold water if necessary. Turn out onto a floured work surface and knead briefly. Divide the dough into 12 pieces, roll out each piece into a 12-cm/4½-inch round and use to line the muffin holes. Chill for 30 minutes. Meanwhile, heat the oil in a saucepan over a low heat and cook the leek and courgette until soft.

Remove the muffin tin from the refrigerator and line each pastry case with baking paper and baking beans. Bake blind in the preheated oven for 10 minutes, then remove from the oven. Lift out the paper and beans. Divide the vegetable mixture between the pastry cases, top with the ham and sprinkle with the cheese.

Reduce the oven temperature to 180°C/350°F/Gas Mark 4. Whisk 2 eggs with the milk in a bowl, season to taste with pepper and pour into the pastry cases. Bake in the oven for 18–20 minutes until golden. Remove from the oven and leave to cool in the tin.

100 g/3½ oz unsalted butter, diced and chilled, plus extra for greasing

125 g/4½ oz white plain flour, plus extra for dusting

100 g/3½ oz wholemeal plain flour

1 egg yolk

1 tbsp olive oil

1 leek, finely chopped

1 courgette, finely sliced

4 slices thin ham, chopped

50 g/1¾ oz Gruyère or Cheddar cheese, grated

2 large eggs

200 ml/7 fl oz full-fat milk

sea salt and pepper

Coconut Muesli Squares

125 g/4½ oz unsalted butter,
softened, plus extra for greasing

75 g/2¾ oz light brown muscovado
sugar

1 egg yolk

125 g/4½ oz wholemeal plain flour

25 g/1 oz no-added-sugar
custard powder

6 tbsp honey

125 g/4½ oz rolled oats

50 g/1¾ oz unsweetened
desiccated coconut

75 g/2¾ oz dried mango, chopped

25 g/1 oz shelled Brazil nuts,
chopped

Preheat the oven to 190°C/375°F/Gas Mark 5. Take a 22-cm/8½-inch square baking tin that is 3 cm/1¼ inches deep, and grease and line it.

Beat 100 g/3½ oz softened butter with the sugar and egg yolk, using an electric mixer, or by hand, until light and fluffy. Fold in the flour and custard powder and mix well. Spoon the mixture into the baking tin, level the surface and bake in the preheated oven for 15 minutes.

Meanwhile, melt the remaining butter and 5 tablespoons of the honey in a small saucepan over a low heat. Put the oats, coconut, mango and nuts in a bowl, add the melted butter and honey and stir to combine.

Remove the baking tin from the oven and spread the sponge with the remaining honey. Top with the coconut mixture and press down well. Return to the oven and bake for a further 15 minutes.

Remove from the oven and leave to cool in the tin, then cut into 16 squares.

Makes 20

Tuna Bites

Mash the tuna with the egg, parsley, a pinch of salt, and pepper to taste. Add the breadcrumbs and mix well, then add enough of the flour to bind the mixture together.

Divide the mixture into 20 mini portions, shape each portion into a ball and chill for 15 minutes.

Meanwhile, preheat the oven to 190°C/375°F/ Gas Mark 5. Brush a non-stick baking sheet with a little oil. Space the tuna balls out on the baking sheet and brush with a little more oil. Bake in the preheated oven for 15–20 minutes until golden and crisp.

Remove from the oven and drain on kitchen paper. Serve warm or cold.

200 g/7 oz canned tuna in spring
water, drained
1 egg
1 tsp finely chopped fresh parsley
50 g/1¾ oz fresh wholemeal
breadcrumbs
about 1 tbsp wholemeal plain flour
vegetable oil, for brushing
sea salt and pepper

Makes 10

Strawberry Cupcakes

Preheat the oven to 180°C/350°F/Gas Mark 4. Line 10 holes of a muffin tin with cake paper cases.

Beat the butter with the sugars in a bowl until pale and fluffy, then beat in the vanilla extract. Add half the egg and beat well.

In a separate bowl, mix the flours and cinnamon together, then add half to the butter mixture and stir to combine. Add the remaining egg and flour mixture and stir to combine. Add the mashed strawberries and mix well.

Spoon the mixture into the paper cases and bake in the preheated oven for 15 minutes. Remove from the oven and leave to cool on a wire rack.

Just before serving, spread thinly with the mascarpone cheese and top with a strawberry half or a whole wild strawberry.

125 g/4½ oz unsalted butter, softened
75 g/2¾ oz unrefined caster sugar
50 g/1¾ oz demerara sugar
1 tsp vanilla extract
2 large eggs, beaten
75 g/2¾ oz white self-raising flour
50 g/1¾ oz light brown self-raising flour
½ tsp ground cinnamon
2 large strawberries, mashed
5 strawberries, halved, or 10 whole wild strawberries
3 tbsp mascarpone cheese

Pinwheel Sandwiches

Fillings

finely mashed canned tuna
   and mayonnaise

cream cheese and finely chopped
   wafer-thin ham

finely mashed egg and mayonnaise

Marmite™ or Vegemite™

goat's cheese and mashed avocado
   (add a little lemon juice to
   prevent avocado discolouring)

grated cheese

mashed canned sardines and
   cream cheese

thinly sliced cooked turkey
   with cranberry sauce

no-added-sugar or -salt peanut
   butter or other nut butters

Swiss cheese and chutney

ricotta cheese and honey

hummus

These are great party sandwiches, because kids like their shape and size and the fact that they don't look like normal sandwiches. Using wholemeal or Granary bread is the healthy option.

To make 6 pinwheels, you will need 1 slice of bread, with the crusts removed, plus the filling. Mash the filling with a little softened butter and spread over the bread. Starting with the short end, tightly roll up into a sausage shape. Repeat with more slices of bread and then chill for 15–20 minutes. Remove from the refrigerator and, using a sharp knife, cut each 'sausage' into 6 slices. To make the pinwheels neat and appealing, avoid using chunky fillings. Choose from the healthy fillings shown here.

Cheese Star Biscuits

150 g/5½ oz butter, softened

175 g/6 oz Parmesan cheese,
  finely grated

50 g/1¾ oz mature Cheddar
  cheese, finely grated

100 g/3½ oz plain flour, plus
  extra for dusting

75 g/2¾ oz wholemeal plain flour

pinch of celery salt or sea salt

1 egg yolk

1 tbsp olive oil

2 tbsp full-fat milk

25 g/1 oz sesame seeds or linseeds

Beat the butter with the cheeses in a bowl until well combined. Add the flours and salt and stir to combine. Mix in the egg yolk and oil to form a soft dough. Wrap the dough in clingfilm and chill for 30 minutes.

Meanwhile, preheat the oven to 180°C/350°F/Gas Mark 4.

Remove the dough from the refrigerator, unwrap it and roll it out on a floured work surface. Using a star-shaped pastry cutter, cut out 35 stars, re-rolling the trimmings where possible.

Place the biscuits on a non-stick baking sheet, brush with the milk and scatter over the seeds. Bake in the preheated oven for 12–15 minutes until golden. Remove from the oven and leave to cool on a wire rack.

Party Straws

Use brightly coloured straws rather than sticks to thread inviting and colourful morsels of food – each child could have 2 or 3 straws in a cup and you could perhaps offer an accompanying dip such as guacamole. You can make both savoury and sweet straws, and obviously the more variety there is the better. Use a metal skewer to make a hole in each piece of food and thread onto the straws. Try the suggestions listed here or use your child's favourite foods.

Savoury Straws

rolled up strips of cooked chicken, turkey, ham, salami or pastrami

cherry tomatoes

radishes

cubes of hard cheese

individual mozzarella cheese balls

cooked lean organic sausage

mini gherkins, halved

baby sweetcorn

baby carrots, halved

squares of Spanish Omelette

cooked chicken breast, cubed

silverskin onions

Sweet Straws

whole raspberries

halved or whole strawberries

chunks of banana, pineapple, mango or pawpaw

kiwi fruit or melon, cubed

dried fruit, cut into bite-sized pieces

stoned cherries

seedless grapes

mandarin segments

stoned lychees

With increasingly hectic lives, it is sometimes difficult to assemble the family together for a meal. However, it is very important for kids to eat with the family, not only to develop their social skills, but also to learn by example – if you are eating healthily, it is far more likely that your children will do so. It is equally important to offer children a wide range of foods and encourage them to try new ones. Growing children need a good balance of all the food groups, and it is particularly vital to include as wide a variety as possible of fruit and vegetables for optimum vitamin and mineral intake, as well as 'good' fats and oils. No food should be off-limits, but those high in saturated fats, sugar and salt should not feature heavily in your child's diet. And remember to avoid falling into the trap of using food as a bribe, because this places an emphasis and importance on certain foods – usually the unhealthy ones! It is crucial that kids don't develop the idea that some foods are more important or desirable than others.

5 family meals

Eating healthily will benefit everyone and the recipes in this chapter offer an opportunity for all the family to enjoy good, nutritious food. There are some straightforward ways to improve the nutritional value of certain foods by simply adapting them – for instance, if your kids love pasta, make a Roast Vegetable Lasagne with five or six different vegetables instead of meat. Try to add vegetables whenever possible and use pulses to bulk up traditionally meat-based recipes. Vary the types of foods you prepare throughout the week for maximum nutritional benefit and to maintain your child's interest in food and cooking.

Easy Scone Pizzas

2 tbsp olive oil, plus extra
   for oiling

1 onion, chopped

800 g/1 lb 12 oz canned chopped
   tomatoes, drained

1 tsp tomato purée

1 tbsp fresh thyme leaves

1 red pepper, deseeded and
   thinly sliced

1 yellow pepper, deseeded and
   thinly sliced

1 courgette, thinly sliced

250 g/9 oz baby spinach leaves

200 g/7 oz wholemeal plain flour

250 g/9 oz white plain flour,
   plus extra for dusting

1 tsp demerara sugar

1 tsp bicarbonate of soda

1 tsp sea salt

350 ml/12 fl oz buttermilk

3 slices ham, chopped

250 g/9 oz mozzarella,
   thinly sliced

pepper

Heat half the oil in a large frying pan and cook the onion for 5 minutes until soft but not browned. Add the tomatoes, tomato purée and thyme and season to taste with pepper. Simmer for 30 minutes until you have a thick sauce with almost no liquid. Remove from the frying pan and leave to cool.

Heat the remaining oil in the frying pan and cook the peppers and courgette for 5–8 minutes until just beginning to brown. Leave to cool.

Put the spinach in a colander and pour boiling water from a kettle over the leaves to wilt. Leave to cool, then squeeze all the liquid out until the spinach is very dry. Chop finely.

Preheat the oven to 220°C/425°F/Gas Mark 7. Lightly oil 2 baking sheets. Put the flours, sugar, bicarbonate of soda and salt in a large bowl, add the buttermilk and mix well to form a dough. Turn out onto a floured work surface and knead briefly.

Divide the dough into 6 pieces, roll out each piece into a 13-cm/5-inch round and place on the prepared baking sheets. Spread the pizza bases with the tomato sauce, then top with the spinach, peppers, courgette, ham and cheese. Bake in the preheated oven for 25 minutes.

Remove from the oven and serve.

Burritos

1 tbsp olive oil

1 onion, chopped

1 garlic clove, finely chopped

500 g/1 lb 2 oz extra-lean fresh
   beef mince

3 large tomatoes, deseeded and
   chopped

1 red pepper, deseeded and
   chopped

½ red chilli, finely chopped
   (optional)

400 g/14 oz canned no-added-salt
   mixed pulses, drained

400 g/14 oz canned no-added-salt
   red kidney beans, drained

125 ml/4 fl oz low-salt vegetable
   stock

1 tbsp finely chopped fresh parsley

8 wholemeal flour tortillas

125 ml/4 fl oz passata

50 g/1¾ oz Cheddar cheese, grated

3 spring onions, sliced

sea salt and pepper

mixed salad, to serve

Heat the oil in a large, non-stick frying pan and cook the onion and garlic until the onion is soft but not browned. Remove from the pan with a slotted spoon. Add the mince and cook over a high heat, breaking up with a wooden spoon, for 3–4 minutes until beginning to brown. Drain off any excess oil.

Return the onion and garlic to the frying pan, add the tomatoes and red peppers, and chilli if using, and cook for 8–10 minutes. Add the pulses, kidney beans, stock and parsley, season to taste with salt and pepper and cook, uncovered, for a further 20–30 minutes until well thickened. Meanwhile, preheat the oven to 180°C/350°F/Gas Mark 4.

Mash the meat mixture to break up the beans, then divide between the tortillas. Roll each one up and place, seam-side down, in a baking dish.

Pour the passata over the burritos and sprinkle over the cheese. Bake in the preheated oven for 20 minutes. Remove from the oven, scatter over the spring onions and serve with a mixed salad.

Makes 12

Salmon Fishcakes

Preheat the oven to 200°C/400°F/Gas Mark 6. Put the salmon in a saucepan with the milk and bay leaf and bring slowly up to simmering point. Simmer for 2 minutes, then remove the saucepan from the heat, lift out and discard the bay leaf and leave the fish in the milk to cool. When cool, lift out the fish with a slotted spoon onto kitchen paper to drain.

Flake the fish into a large bowl. Put the broccoli in a food processor and pulse until smooth. Add to the fish with the mashed potatoes, the parsley, 1 tablespoon of the flour, and pepper to taste. Add the egg yolk and mix well. If the mixture is a little dry, add some of the poaching milk; if too wet, add a little more flour.

Divide the mixture into 12 portions and shape each portion into a cake. Put the beaten eggs, remaining flour and the breadcrumbs on 3 separate plates. Roll each fishcake in the flour, then in the beaten egg, and then in the breadcrumbs to coat.

Heat the oil in a non-stick baking tray in the preheated oven for 5 minutes. Add the fishcakes and bake for 10 minutes, then carefully turn the fishcakes over and bake for a further 10 minutes.

700 g/1 lb 9 oz skinless salmon
    fillet, cut into cubes
300 ml/10 fl oz full-fat milk
1 bay leaf
100 g/3½ oz broccoli, steamed
    until tender
700 g/1 lb 9 oz potatoes, boiled
    and mashed
2 tbsp finely chopped fresh parsley
4 tbsp wholemeal plain flour
1 egg yolk
2 large eggs, beaten
150 g/5½ oz fresh wholemeal
    breadcrumbs
2 tbsp olive oil
pepper

Sweet Potato, Cheese and Leek Pie

2 tbsp olive oil

2 garlic cloves, finely chopped

200 ml/7 fl oz crème fraîche

1.3 kg/3 lb sweet potatoes,
   peeled and thinly sliced

1 tsp butter, plus extra for
   greasing

2 leeks, finely sliced

75 g/2¾ oz Gruyère cheese, grated

25 g/1 oz fresh wholemeal
   breadcrumbs

pepper

Preheat the oven to 190°C/375°F/Gas Mark 5. Mix the oil, garlic and crème fraîche together in a large bowl, add the sweet potato slices and toss until well coated.

Melt the butter in a non-stick frying pan and cook the leeks until soft. Add to the sweet potatoes and mix until evenly distributed. Season to taste with pepper.

Lightly grease a gratin dish. Layer in the sweet potato mixture and top with the cheese and breadcrumbs.

Cover with foil and bake in the preheated oven for 1 hour, removing the foil for the last 5 minutes of the cooking time.

Serves 4

Sausage and Bean Casserole

Preheat the oven to 180°C/350°F/Gas Mark 4. Heat the oil in a non-stick frying pan and briefly brown the sausages. Remove from the pan with a slotted spoon and drain on kitchen paper. Add the onion and red pepper to the frying pan and cook until soft, then add the tomatoes and simmer for a further 2–3 minutes.

Add the pulses, passata, parsley and tomato purée, and salt and pepper to taste, and cook for 5 minutes.

Spoon the pulses and sauce into a casserole dish and add the sausages. Cover and cook in the preheated oven for 25 minutes.

Remove from the oven and serve hot with a swirl of yogurt.

1 tbsp olive oil

8 lean organic pork sausages

1 onion, finely chopped

1 red pepper, deseeded and chopped

6 tomatoes, deseeded and chopped

1.2 kg/2 lb 10 oz canned no-salt-added mixed pulses, drained

600 ml/1 pint passata

1 tbsp chopped fresh parsley

1 tbsp tomato purée

3 tbsp natural yogurt

sea salt and pepper

Serves 4

Shepherd's Pie

Heat half the oil in a non-stick frying pan and cook the mince over a high heat, breaking up with a wooden spoon, until well browned. Remove the mince from the pan with a slotted spoon, pour away any fat and wipe the pan with kitchen paper.

Add the remaining oil to the frying pan and cook the leek, onion, carrots and celery for 15 minutes until soft. Return the mince to the pan and add the mushrooms, tomatoes, thyme and water. Season to taste with salt and pepper and leave to simmer for 40 minutes, stirring occasionally.

Meanwhile, preheat the oven to 180°C/350°F/Gas Mark 4. Mix the 2 mashes of potatoes with half the milk and half the butter in a bowl and season to taste with salt and pepper.

Spoon the meat sauce into a baking dish and top with the potato mixture. Brush with the remaining milk and dot with the remaining butter. Bake in the preheated oven for 35 minutes until the topping is brown and crisp.

2 tbsp olive oil
750 g/1 lb 10 oz lean fresh
   lamb mince
1 leek, chopped
1 small red onion, chopped
2 carrots, chopped
1 celery stick, chopped
100 g/3½ oz mushrooms, chopped
400 g/14 oz canned tomatoes
2 tbsp fresh thyme leaves
125 ml/4 fl oz water
500 g/1 lb 2 oz potatoes,
   boiled and mashed
400 g/14 oz sweet potatoes,
   boiled and mashed
4 tbsp milk
knob of unsalted butter
sea salt and pepper

Roast Vegetable Lasagne

3 tbsp olive oil

4 courgettes, halved lengthways and thickly sliced

3 red peppers, deseeded and chopped

1 aubergine, chopped

2 red onions, chopped

5 shallots, peeled and quartered

250 g/9 oz button mushrooms

400 g/14 oz canned chopped tomatoes

1 tbsp tomato purée

50 g/1¾ oz butter

50 g/1¾ oz plain flour or gluten-free flour

600 ml/1 pint full-fat milk

100 g/3½ oz Cheddar cheese, grated

200 g/7 oz fresh lasagne

2 tbsp grated Parmesan cheese

sea salt and pepper

green salad, to serve

Preheat the oven to 190°C/375°F/Gas Mark 5. Put the oil in a large bowl, add the courgettes, peppers, aubergine, onions and shallots and toss well to coat.

Divide the vegetables between 2 baking trays and roast in the preheated oven for 30–40 minutes until soft and flecked with brown. Add the button mushrooms after 20 minutes.

Remove the vegetables from the oven and tip into a large bowl. Add the tomatoes and tomato purée and mix well.

Melt the butter in a saucepan over a low heat. Stir in the flour and cook, stirring constantly, for 2–3 minutes. Gradually add the milk and cook, continuing to stir constantly, until the sauce is thick and smooth. Season to taste with salt and pepper and stir in the Cheddar cheese.

Layer the vegetable mixture and sauce in an ovenproof dish with the lasagne, finishing with a layer of sauce. Sprinkle over the Parmesan cheese and bake in the oven for 30–35 minutes.

Remove from the oven and serve hot with a green salad.

Roasted Chicken and Sweet Potatoes

8 organic chicken thighs, skinned

1 red onion, finely chopped

8 tbsp low-sugar and -salt tomato
 ketchup

2 tbsp maple syrup

1 tbsp Worcestershire sauce

1 tbsp coarse-grain mustard

1 garlic clove, finely chopped

3 tbsp olive oil

4 sweet potatoes, cut into chunks

Preheat the oven to 200°C/400°F/Gas Mark 6. Score each chicken thigh 2–3 times.

Mix all the remaining ingredients, except the sweet potatoes, together in a large bowl. Add the chicken and toss well to coat. Cover with clingfilm and leave to marinate in a cool place for 20 minutes, then add the sweet potatoes and toss well to coat.

Tip the chicken and sweet potatoes into a baking dish and roast in the preheated oven for 40–50 minutes until well browned. The chicken should be tender and the juices run clear when a skewer is inserted into the thickest part of the meat.

The chicken thighs and sweet potatoes could also be cooked on a barbecue in the summer.

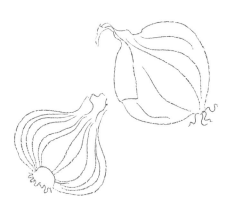

Serves 4

Chicken and Leek Pie

Put the chicken, onion, carrot, celery and herbs in a flameproof casserole and cover with cold water. Cover and bring to the boil, then reduce the heat and simmer for 1 hour, or until the chicken is tender and the juices run clear when a skewer is inserted into the thickest part of the meat. Remove the chicken from the casserole. Discard the skin. Remove the meat from the carcass, cut into chunks and reserve. Sieve the chicken cooking liquid, discarding the vegetables and herbs, and reserve.

Preheat the oven to 190°C/375°F/Gas Mark 5. Heat the oil in a large frying pan and cook the onion until soft but not browned. Remove from the pan with a slotted spoon and set aside. Melt the butter in the frying pan and cook the leeks for 5 minutes. Stir in the flour and cook, stirring constantly, for 2–3 minutes. Gradually add 425 ml/15 fl oz of the reserved cooking liquid and cook, continuing to stir constantly, until the sauce is thick and smooth. Stir in the mushrooms and ham. Mix the cooked chicken with the onion and the sauce and stir in the cream. Season to taste with salt and pepper and spoon into a baking dish.

Brush each sheet of filo pastry with a little of the vegetable oil, then scrunch up and place over the chicken mixture. Bake in the preheated oven for 30 minutes until the filo pastry topping is brown and crisp.

1 organic chicken, weighing
 1.3 kg/3 lb
1 onion, quartered
1 carrot, cut into chunks
1 celery stick, cut into chunks
1 bay leaf
1 fresh rosemary sprig
3 tbsp olive oil
1 red onion, chopped
25 g/1 oz butter
3 leeks, sliced
25 g/1 oz plain or gluten-free flour
250 g/9 oz field or chestnut
 mushrooms, halved
100 g/3½ oz ham, sliced
3 tbsp double cream
4 sheets filo pastry, thawed if
 frozen
2 tbsp vegetable oil
sea salt and pepper

Makes 12 slices

Apple Cake

Preheat the oven to 180°C/350°F/Gas Mark 4. Grease and line a 23-cm/9-inch round cake tin. Arrange the apple slices in the bottom of the prepared tin.

Put all the remaining ingredients, except the honey and dried apple, in a food processor and pulse until well combined. Pour the cake mixture over the apples and bake in the preheated oven for 1 hour until cooked through – a skewer inserted into the centre of the cake should come out clean.

Remove from the oven and leave to cool in the tin, then invert onto a plate and remove the lining paper. Turn back over onto a serving plate. Spread the top of the cake with the honey and scatter over the dried apple. Cut into 12 equal pieces.

225 g/8 oz unsalted butter, diced, plus extra for greasing

3 apples, peeled, cored and sliced

100 g/3½ oz unrefined caster sugar

100 g/3½ oz demerara sugar

½ tsp vanilla extract

½ tsp ground cinnamon

4 large eggs

100 g/3½ oz light brown self-raising flour

125 g/4½ oz white self-raising flour

1 tsp baking powder

1 tbsp clear honey

3–4 slices dried apple, chopped

Raspberry Fool

300 g/10½ oz fresh raspberries,
   plus extra to decorate
225 g/8 oz natural or Greek-style
   yogurt
1 tbsp clear honey
1 egg white
50 g/1¾ oz toasted flaked almonds

Put the raspberries in a blender or food processor and process until smooth. Pour the purée through a fine nylon sieve to remove the seeds, then fold into the yogurt in a large bowl. Stir in the honey.

In a separate grease-free bowl, whisk the egg white until beginning to stiffen, then fold into the raspberry mixture.

Spoon into individual glasses, cover with clingfilm, and chill for 3 hours. Scatter over the almonds and the extra fresh raspberries before serving.

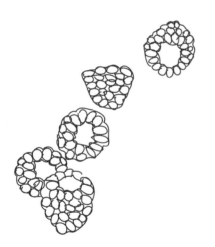

Serves 4

Plum Crisp

Preheat the oven to 180°C/350°F/Gas Mark 4. Arrange the plums in the bottom of a baking dish.

Put the oats, almonds, nuts, honey and sugar in a bowl. Melt the butter in a small saucepan over a low heat, pour into the oat mixture and stir to combine. Spoon over the plums. Bake in the preheated oven for 35 minutes.

Remove the dish from the oven and serve hot with Greek-style yogurt.

750 g/1 lb 10 oz ripe plums,
    stoned and halved
75 g/2¾ oz jumbo oats
50 g/1¾ oz flaked almonds
50 g/1¾ oz shelled pecan nuts,
    chopped
4 tbsp clear honey
2 tbsp demerara sugar
50 g/1¾ oz unsalted butter
Greek-style yogurt, to serve

Crispy Vegetable Bake

Preheat the oven to 190°C/375°F/Gas Mark 5. Grease a 20-cm/8-inch round baking dish with butter.

Cook the potato slices in a large saucepan of boiling water for 5 minutes. Drain and cover with a clean tea towel to absorb the steam.

Melt half the butter with 1 tablespoon of the oil in a large frying pan and cook the garlic, oregano and leek for 3–4 minutes. Remove with a slotted spoon and transfer to a plate. Add the remaining oil to the frying pan and cook the parsnips, carrots and celeriac for 10 minutes until soft and cooked through. Season to taste with salt and pepper and cook for a further 5 minutes. Stir in the leek mixture.

Arrange half the potato slices in the bottom of the prepared dish, top with half the vegetable mixture and then sprinkle over half the cheese. Cover with the remaining vegetable mixture and cheese and top with the remaining potato slices. Dot with the remaining butter and bake in the preheated oven for 40 minutes until golden and crisp.

Five minutes before serving, poach the eggs. Serve the vegetable bake topped with the poached eggs, accompanied by a green salad.

25 g/1 oz butter, plus extra
   for greasing
750 g/1 lb 10 oz potatoes,
   thinly sliced
3 tbsp olive oil
1 garlic clove, crushed
1 tsp fresh oregano leaves
1 large leek, shredded
2 parsnips, peeled and grated
3 carrots, peeled and grated
½ head celeriac, peeled and grated
200 g/7 oz feta cheese, crumbled
4 eggs
sea salt and pepper
green salad, to serve

Winter Fruit and Nut Crumble

1.3 kg/3 lb Bramley apples, peeled,
   cored and chopped, or a
   mixture of apples and quinces

1 tbsp water

3 tbsp clear honey

250 g/9 oz blackberries

25 g/1 oz unsalted butter

2 tbsp demerara sugar

3 tbsp wholemeal plain flour

200 g/7 oz rolled oats

1 tsp ground nutmeg

2 tbsp toasted hazelnuts, chopped

half-fat fromage frais, to serve

Preheat the oven to 190°C/375°F/Gas Mark 5. Put the apples in a saucepan with the water and 1 tablespoon of the honey over a medium heat. Cook for 10 minutes. Leave to cool, then mix with the blackberries. Arrange the fruit mixture in the bottom of a baking dish.

Melt the butter in a small saucepan over a low heat. Leave to cool slightly. Meanwhile, mix all the remaining ingredients together in a large bowl. Pour in the melted butter and stir to combine. Spoon over the fruit mixture in the dish.

Bake in the preheated oven for 35–40 minutes. Serve hot with half-fat fromage frais.

Serves 4

Banana Cinnamon Bread and Butter Pudding

Preheat the oven to 180°C/350°F/Gas Mark 4. Lightly grease a baking dish and arrange the banana slices in the bottom. Top with the bread slices, overlapping each slice to cover the banana.

Whisk the sugar, eggs, milk and cinnamon together in a bowl and pour over the bread.

Drizzle over the honey and bake in the preheated oven for 30–40 minutes until risen and golden.

unsalted butter, for greasing

2 bananas, peeled and sliced

8 slices malted wholegrain bread, lightly buttered and cut in half diagonally, crusts removed

2 tbsp demerara sugar

3 large eggs

300 ml/10 fl oz full-fat milk

1½ tsp ground cinnamon

2 tbsp clear honey

A great way to develop your children's positive interest in food is to involve them, when you can, in preparing and cooking it, and no matter how young they are, there is invariably some way in which they can participate. It takes very little effort to introduce children to the basics of good food, and they are much more likely to try a dish if they have been involved in making it than if it simply appears on a plate in front of them. This chapter offers recipes that are not only fun for children to help you make, but are really delicious to eat and healthy, too.

6 treats

Needless to say, it is virtually impossible to insulate children against the might of the fast-food giants, but if they really do want burgers and chicken nuggets, then make them bean burgers and home-made nuggets. You can usually find a way of making healthier, home-made versions of fast-food menu items. Chocolate is another obvious pull for kids, but as no food should be off-limits, find ways of including it in a limited way and in conjunction with some fruit, because this is a good source of antioxidants, and choose chocolate with a high proportion of cocoa solids (70%).

Children love food that is presented in an attractive and colourful way, and you can use this to encourage your child to choose the healthy option. Chop fruit and vegetables into fun shapes and utilize novelty biscuit cutters. Serve food on paper plates showing their favourite cartoon characters, and present healthy snacks in unusual ways, such as chopped fruit and nuts in little pots or mini boxes. Make healthy food a treat through the variety and originality of its presentation.

Spicy Bean Burgers

Mash the beans with a potato masher in a bowl until they are smooth, then add the pesto, breadcrumbs, egg, a pinch of salt, and pepper to taste, and mix well.

Heat half the oil in a non-stick frying pan over a low heat and cook the onion and garlic until soft. Add to the bean mixture and mix well.

Heat the remaining oil in the frying pan. Spoon in the bean mixture, in 6 separate mounds, then press each one down with the back of a spoon to form a burger.

Cook the burgers for 4–5 minutes, then carefully turn over and cook for a further 4–5 minutes until golden.

Meanwhile, slice the rolls in half and smear each one with the hummus.

Remove the burgers from the frying pan and drain on kitchen paper. Place each one in a roll, top with the tomatoes, cucumber and salad leaves and serve.

400 g/14 oz canned cannellini
    beans, drained and rinsed
2 tbsp red pesto
75 g/2¾ oz fresh wholemeal
    breadcrumbs
1 egg
2 tbsp olive oil
½ small red onion, finely chopped
1 garlic clove, crushed
6 Granary rolls
6 tsp hummus
pepper
sea salt

To serve
2 cherry tomatoes, sliced
cucumber or cornichons, sliced
green salad leaves

Serves 4

Chicken Nuggets

Preheat the oven to 190°C/375°F/Gas Mark 5. Cut the chicken breasts into 4-cm/1½-inch chunks. Mix the flour, wheatgerm, cumin, coriander, and pepper to taste, in a bowl, then divide in half and put on 2 separate plates. Put the beaten egg on a third plate.

Pour the oil into a baking tray and heat in the oven. Roll the chicken pieces in one plate of flour, shake to remove any excess, then roll in the egg and in the second plate of flour, again shaking off any excess flour. When all the nuggets are ready, remove the baking tray from the oven and toss the nuggets in the hot oil. Roast in the oven for 25–30 minutes until golden and crisp.

Meanwhile, to make the dipping sauce, put both kinds of tomatoes in a blender or food processor and process until smooth. Add the mayonnaise and process again until well combined.

Remove the nuggets from the oven and drain on kitchen paper. Serve with the dipping sauce and a green salad.

3 organic skinless, boneless
    chicken breasts
4 tbsp wholemeal plain flour
1 tbsp wheatgerm
½ tsp ground cumin
½ tsp ground coriander
1 egg, lightly beaten
2 tbsp olive oil
100 g/3½ oz sunblush tomatoes
100 g/3½ oz fresh tomatoes,
    peeled, deseeded and chopped
2 tbsp mayonnaise
pepper
green salad, to serve

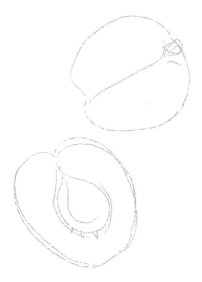

Fruit Skewers

selection of fruit, such as apricots,
    peaches, figs, strawberries,
    mangoes, pineapple, bananas,
    dates and pawpaw, prepared
    and cut into chunks
maple syrup
50 g/1¾ oz plain chocolate
    (minimum 70% cocoa solids),
    broken into chunks

Soak 4 bamboo skewers in water for at least 20 minutes.

Preheat the grill to high and line the grill pan with foil.
Thread alternate pieces of fruit onto each skewer. Brush
the fruit with a little maple syrup.

Put the chocolate in a heatproof bowl, set the bowl over
a saucepan of barely simmering water and heat until
it is melted.

Meanwhile, cook the skewers under the preheated grill for
3 minutes, or until caramelized. Serve drizzled with a little
of the melted chocolate, removing the fruit from the
skewer if serving to younger children.

Makes 6

Cherry Rascals

Preheat the oven to 190°C/375°F/Gas Mark 5. Put the flours, baking powder and butter in a food processor and pulse until the mixture resembles breadcrumbs. Add the sugar, lemon rind, spices and cherries and pulse briefly to mix. Add the egg and milk and pulse again to form a soft dough. Alternatively, mix the flours and baking powder together in a large bowl, add the butter and rub in with your fingertips until the mixture resembles breadcrumbs. Stir in the sugar, lemon rind, spices and cherries, then mix in the egg and milk to form a soft dough. Turn out onto a floured work surface and knead briefly.

Divide the dough into 6 pieces, form each piece into a ball and place on a baking sheet. Press down lightly, brush with milk and sprinkle with the nuts. Bake in the preheated oven for 15 minutes until golden.

Remove from the oven and leave to cool on a wire rack. Serve warm or cold.

75 g/2¾ oz plain flour, plus extra
   for dusting
75 g/2¾ oz light brown self-raising
   flour
½ tsp baking powder
50 g/1¾ oz unsalted butter, diced
   and chilled
50 g/1¾ oz demerara sugar
finely grated rind of 1 lemon
½ tsp ground cinnamon
½ tsp ground nutmeg
75 g/2¾ oz dried cherries
1 egg, beaten
2 tbsp full-fat milk, plus
   extra for brushing
2 tbsp chopped Brazil nuts

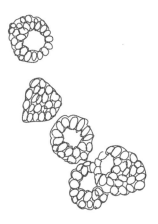

Yogurt Lollies

Put the berries in a blender or food processor and pulse briefly to break them up. Add the yogurt and honey and process to combine.

Pour into six 75 ml/2½ fl oz lolly moulds or plastic cups and insert a lolly stick into each. Freeze for 6 hours.

To unmould, wrap each mould in a hot cloth and carefully lift out the lolly.

300 g/10½ oz frozen mixed berries

400 g/14 oz full-fat natural yogurt

1 tbsp clear honey

Makes 12 slices

Cranberry and Pecan Slices

Preheat the oven to 180°C/350°F/Gas Mark 4. Grease and line a 22-cm/8½-inch square baking tin.

Mix the muesli, cranberries, nuts and sugar together in a large bowl.

Warm the honey in a saucepan over a low heat, then stir into the muesli mixture. Stir in the egg whites and apple juice and mix well.

Spoon the mixture into the prepared baking tin and press down firmly. Bake in the preheated oven for 30 minutes.

Remove from the oven and leave to cool in the tin, then cut into 12 slices.

unsalted butter, for greasing
250 g/9 oz no-added-sugar muesli
75 g/2¾ oz dried cranberries
50 g/1¾ oz shelled pecan nuts, chopped
100 g/3½ oz demerara sugar
3 tbsp clear honey
2 egg whites, lightly beaten
175 ml/6 fl oz apple juice

Mini Strawberry Cheesecakes

75 g/2¾ oz unsalted butter

75 g/2¾ oz rolled oats

25 g/1 oz chopped hazelnuts

225 g/8 oz ricotta cheese

50 g/1¾ oz demerara sugar

finely grated rind of 1 lemon,
 and juice of ½ lemon

1 egg, plus 1 egg yolk

150 g/5½ oz cottage cheese

1 kiwi fruit

6 large strawberries

Line 6 holes of a muffin tin with muffin paper cases.

Melt the butter in a small saucepan over a low heat, then leave to cool. Put the oats in a food processor and pulse briefly to break them up, then tip into a bowl, add the nuts and melted butter and mix well. Divide the mixture between the paper cases and press down well. Chill for 30 minutes.

Preheat the oven to 150°C/300°F/Gas Mark 2. Beat the ricotta cheese with the sugar, and lemon rind and juice, in a bowl. Add the egg, egg yolk and cottage cheese and mix well. Spoon into the muffin cases and bake in the preheated oven for 30 minutes. Turn off the oven, but leave the cheesecakes in the oven until completely cold.

Peel the kiwi fruit and dice the flesh, and slice the strawberries. Remove the paper cases, top each cheesecake with the fruit and serve.

Chocolate Mousse Pots

100 g/3½ oz plain chocolate
(minimum 70% cocoa solids),
chopped

1 tbsp butter

2 large eggs, separated

1 tbsp maple syrup

2 tbsp Greek-style yogurt

100 g/3½ oz blueberries

1 tbsp water

25 g/1 oz white chocolate, grated

Put the chocolate and butter in a heatproof bowl, set the bowl over a saucepan of barely simmering water and heat until melted. Leave to cool slightly, then stir in the egg yolks, maple syrup and yogurt.

Whisk the egg whites in a large, grease-free bowl until stiff, then fold into the chocolate mixture. Divide between 6 small ramekins and chill for 4 hours.

Meanwhile, put the blueberries in a small saucepan with the water and cook until the berries begin to pop and turn glossy. Leave to cool, then chill.

To serve, top each mousse with a few blueberries and a little white chocolate.

Makes 6

Mini Fruit Trifles

Make up the jelly according to the packet instructions.

Divide the fruit between 6 plastic cups or trifle paper cases. Pour over the jelly and chill for 6 hours until firmly set.

Mix the yogurt with the vanilla extract and honey and spoon over the jellies.

Sprinkle with the nuts and serve.

one 12-g/½-oz sachet
    sugar-free jelly
200 g/7 oz fresh fruit, such as
    mangoes, bananas, peaches,
    strawberries, raspberries or
    blueberries, prepared and
    chopped
6 tbsp Greek-style yogurt
1 tsp vanilla extract
3 tbsp clear honey
50 g/1¾ oz shelled pistachio
    nuts, chopped

Makes 1 loaf

Banana Loaf

Preheat the oven to 180°C/350°F/Gas Mark 4. Lightly grease and line a 450-g/1-lb loaf tin.

Sift the flours, sugar, a pinch of salt, and the spices into a large bowl.

In a separate bowl, mash the bananas with the orange juice, then stir in the eggs and oil. Pour into the dry ingredients and mix well.

Spoon into the prepared loaf tin and bake in the preheated oven for 1 hour, then test to see if it is cooked by inserting a skewer into the centre. If it comes out clean, the loaf is done. If not, bake for a further 10 minutes and test again.

Remove from the oven and leave to cool in the tin. Turn the loaf out, slice and serve with honey, and sliced banana or chopped walnuts.

unsalted butter, for greasing
125 g/4½ oz white self-raising flour
100 g/3½ oz light brown
   self-raising flour
150 g/5½ oz demerara sugar
½ tsp ground cinnamon
½ tsp ground nutmeg
2 large ripe bananas, peeled
175 ml/6 fl oz orange juice
2 eggs, beaten
4 tbsp rapeseed oil
sea salt

To serve
honey
sliced banana or chopped walnuts

Baked Banana

Preheat the oven to 190°C/375°F/Gas Mark 5. Make 2 slits along the length of the banana, cutting slightly into the flesh, and pull back the skin, but keep it attached at one end.

Push the chocolate buttons or chocolate flake into the slit and cover with the skin.

Wrap in foil. Keeping it upright, bake it in the preheated oven for 5–10 minutes until the chocolate has melted.

Remove from the foil and serve with yogurt.

1 banana, unpeeled
8 chocolate buttons or half
   a chocolate flake
natural yogurt, to serve

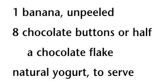

Makes 6

Fruity Filo Parcels

Put the apples, sultanas, nutmeg and maple syrup in a small saucepan over a low heat and cook until the apples are soft. Leave to cool.

Preheat the oven to 190°C/375°F/Gas Mark 5. Cut each sheet of filo pastry in half. Brush one half sparingly with a little oil, place another half on top and brush the edges with a little oil. Spoon some of the apple mixture into the middle, pull in the edges and scrunch to close, to form a little pastry bag. Place on a baking sheet. Repeat with the remaining filo pastry sheets and apple mixture to make 6 parcels.

Brush the tops with a little more oil and bake in the preheated oven for 20 minutes until golden.

Remove from the oven and leave to cool slightly, then serve with yogurt.

3 apples, peeled, cored
   and chopped
2 tbsp sultanas
½ tsp ground nutmeg
1 tbsp maple syrup or honey
6 sheets filo pastry, thawed
   if frozen
groundnut oil, for brushing
natural yogurt, to serve

Sticky Fruit Flapjacks

Preheat the oven to 180°C/350°F/Gas Mark 4. Grease and line a 22-cm/8½-inch square baking tin.

Melt the butter, honey and sugar in a saucepan over a low heat. When the sugar has melted, add the peanut butter and stir until all the ingredients are well combined. Add all the remaining ingredients and mix well.

Press the mixture into the prepared tin and bake in the preheated oven for 20 minutes.

Remove from the oven and leave to cool in the tin, then cut into 16 squares.

175 g/6 oz unsalted butter, plus extra for greasing

3 tbsp clear honey

150 g/5½ oz demerara sugar

100 g/3½ oz no-added-sugar smooth peanut butter

225 g/8 oz porridge oats

50 g/1¾ oz ready-to-eat dried apricots, chopped

2 tbsp sunflower seeds

2 tbsp sesame seeds

Makes 6

Tropical Fruit Tarts

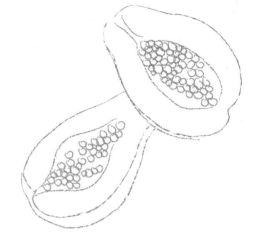

Preheat the oven to 180°C/350°F/Gas Mark 4. Lightly oil 6 holes of a muffin tin.

Cut each sheet of filo pastry into quarters and brush each piece with a little oil. Layer 4 pieces one on top of the other, each at a slightly different angle, then press into a prepared muffin hole to make a rough-edged tart shell. Repeat with the remaining pieces of filo pastry to make 6 tart shells.

Bake in the preheated oven for 10 minutes until golden. Remove from the oven and leave to cool in the tin, then carefully transfer to a serving plate.

Fill each tart shell with the tropical fruit and lychees. Cut each passion fruit in half and scoop out the contents of each half onto a tart. Top with a few coconut curls.

groundnut oil, for oiling
    and brushing
6 sheets filo pastry, thawed
    if frozen
mixed tropical fruit, such as
    pawpaw, mango, pineapple,
    banana, Cape gooseberry,
    prepared and diced
6 lychees, cut into 1-cm/
    ½-inch dice
3 passion fruit
fresh coconut curls

Index